Wallace & Gromit™

Aardman Presents

A Grand Day Out™

First published in 1999 by
BBC Worldwide Ltd, Woodlands,
80 Wood Lane, London, W12 OTT

Illustrated by Bill Kerwin
copyright © Aardman/Wallace & Gromit Ltd 1999
Design copyright © BBC Worldwide Ltd 1999

A Grand Day Out™ copyright © NFTS 1989

Wallace & Gromit™ and copyright
© Wallace & Gromit Ltd 1989
A member of the Aardman group of companies

ISBN 0563 38008 X

Printed and bound in France by
Imprimerie Pollina s.a
Reprographics by Radstock
Reproductions Ltd.

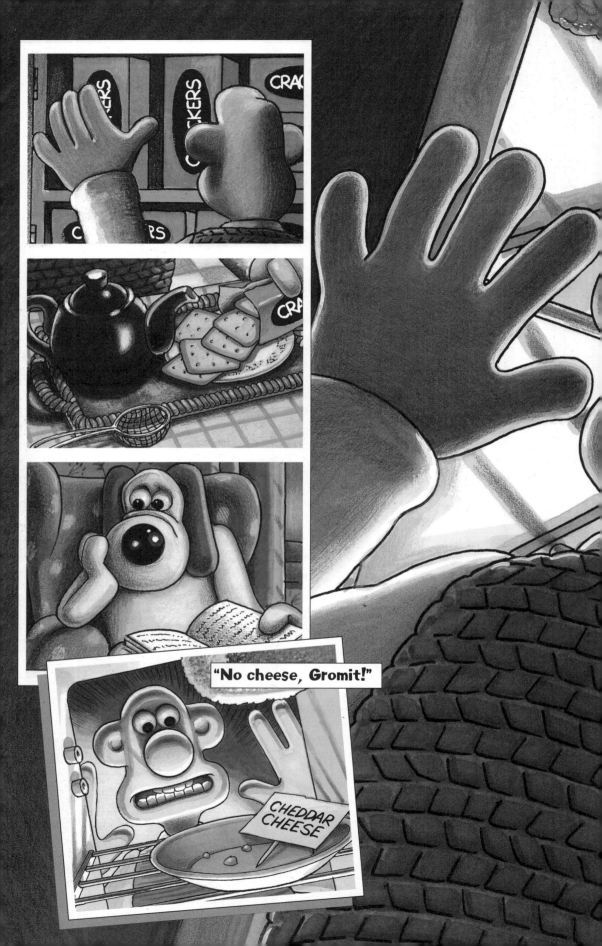

"Everybody knows the Moon's made of cheese."

z-z-z-z-z-Z-Z

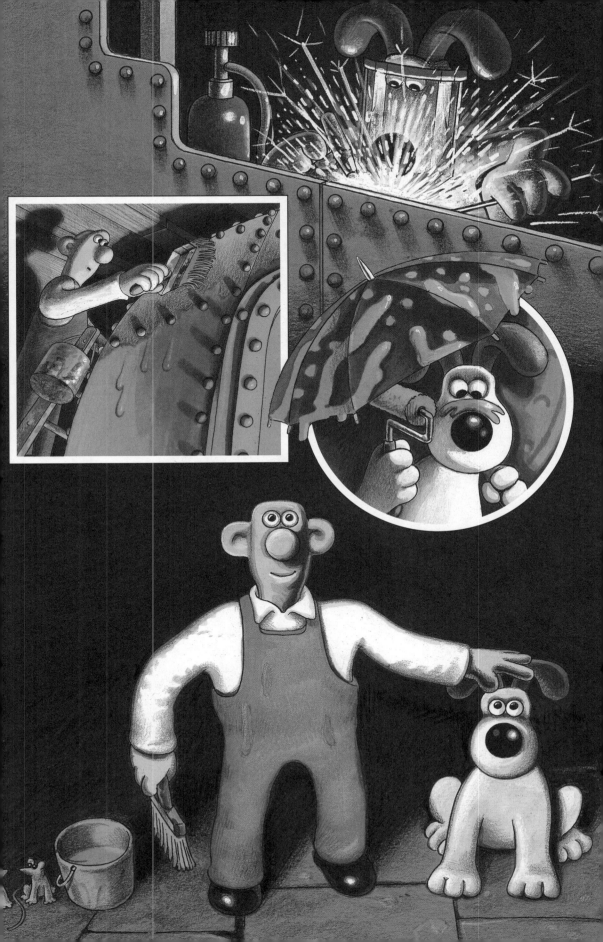

"Ohh!"

"Everything seems to be under control..."

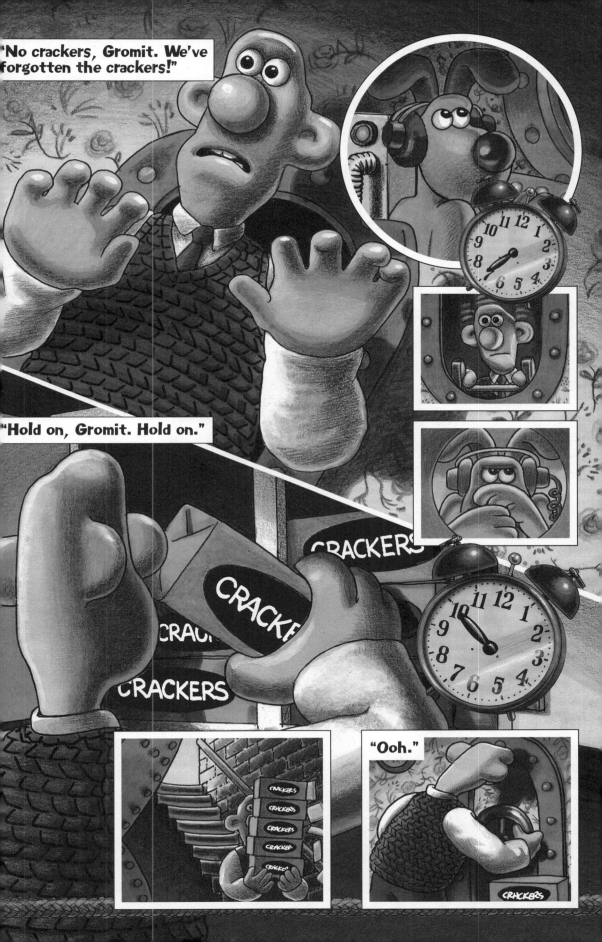

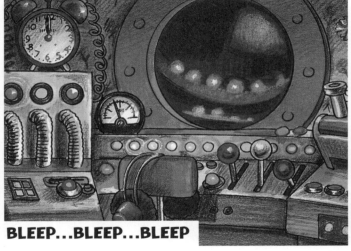

BLEEP...BLEEP...BLEEP

"Hmmm..."

"One for the album."

"Oh, nicely done."

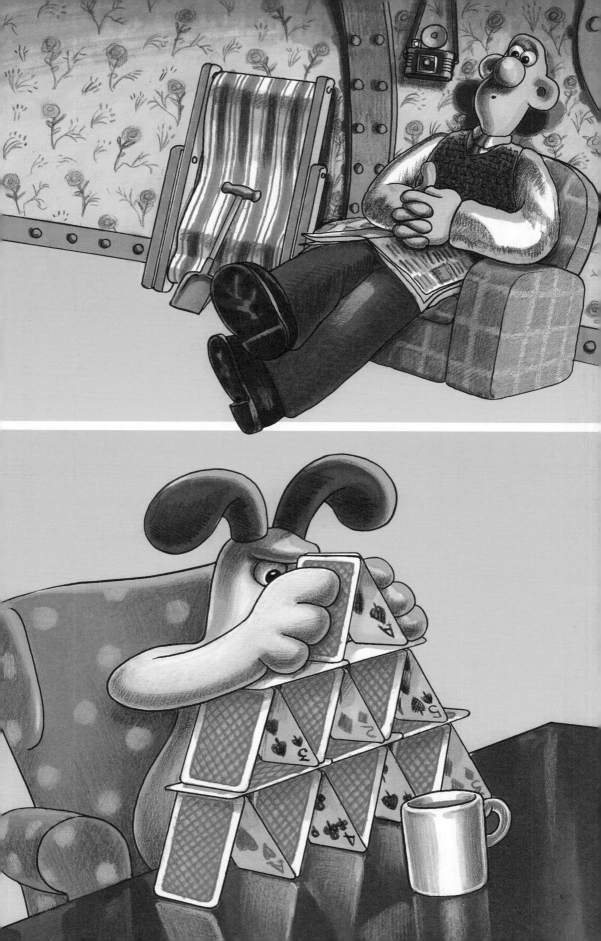

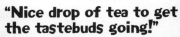

"Wensleydale?"

"Stilton?"

"I don't know, lad. It's like no cheese I've ever tasted."

"See what you think."

"Let's try another spot."

"Hhmmm…"

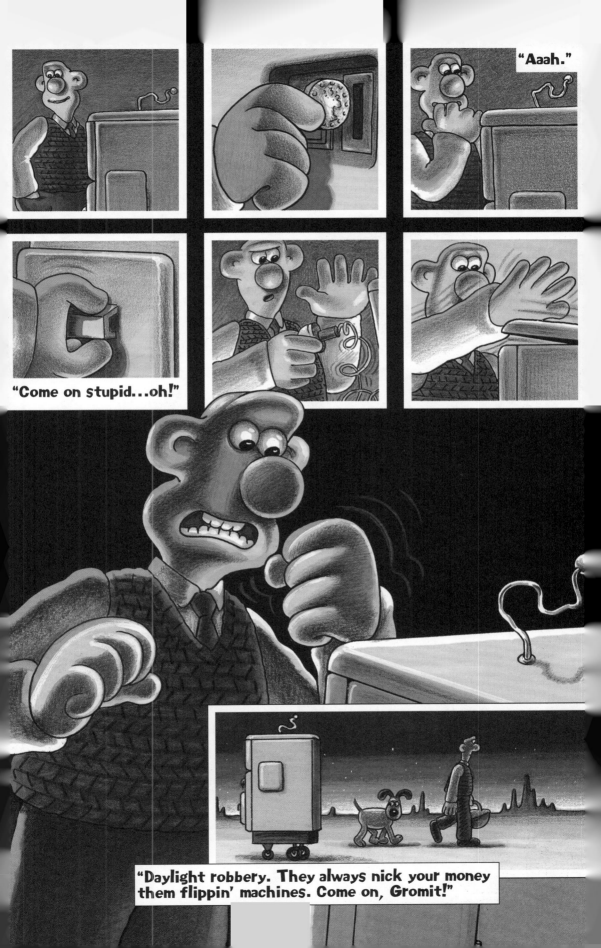

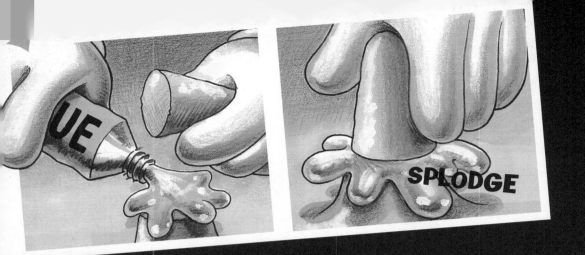

SPLODGE

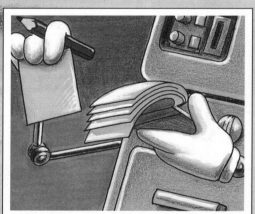

THWACK
THWACK

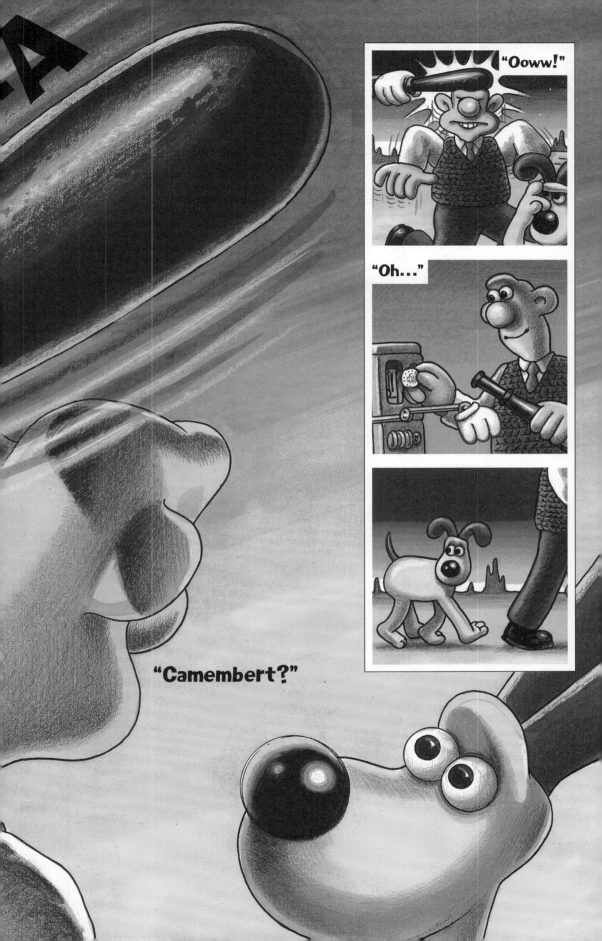

"Emergency countdown!"

"Ten seconds and counting!"

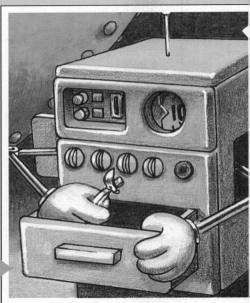

"Hold on tight lad and think of Lancashire hotpot."

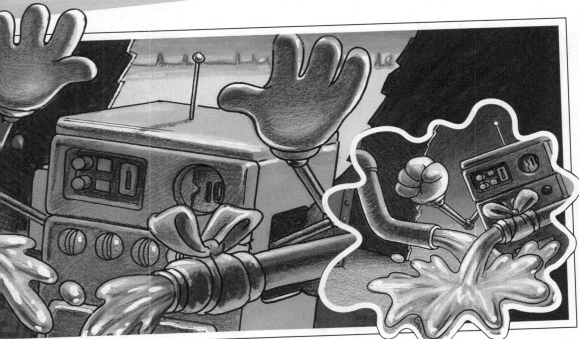

"UHH! AAH!"

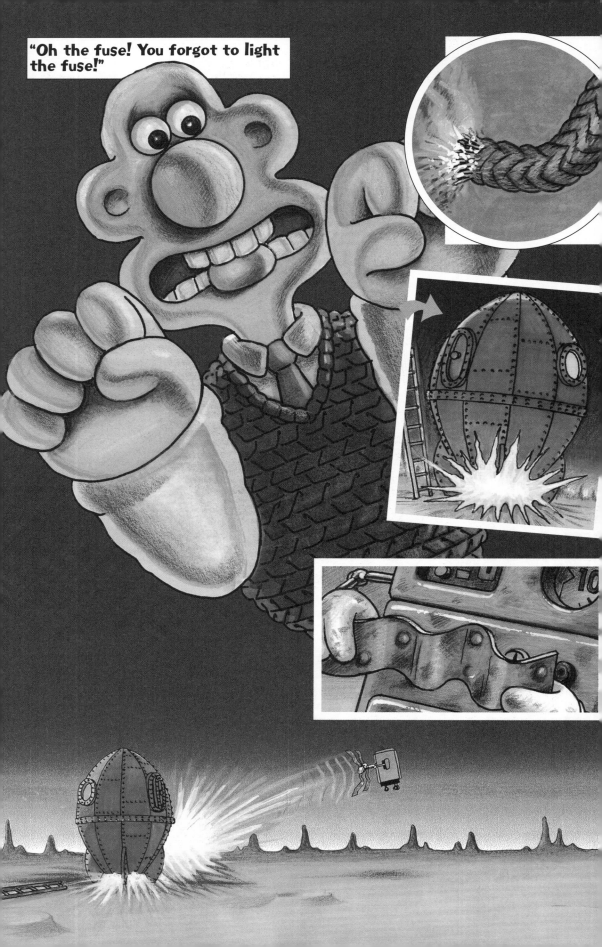

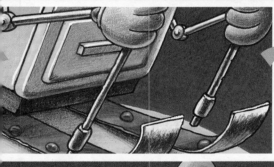